# COLORING BOOKS FOR ADULT

## *Animals For relaxation*

### Horse Collection

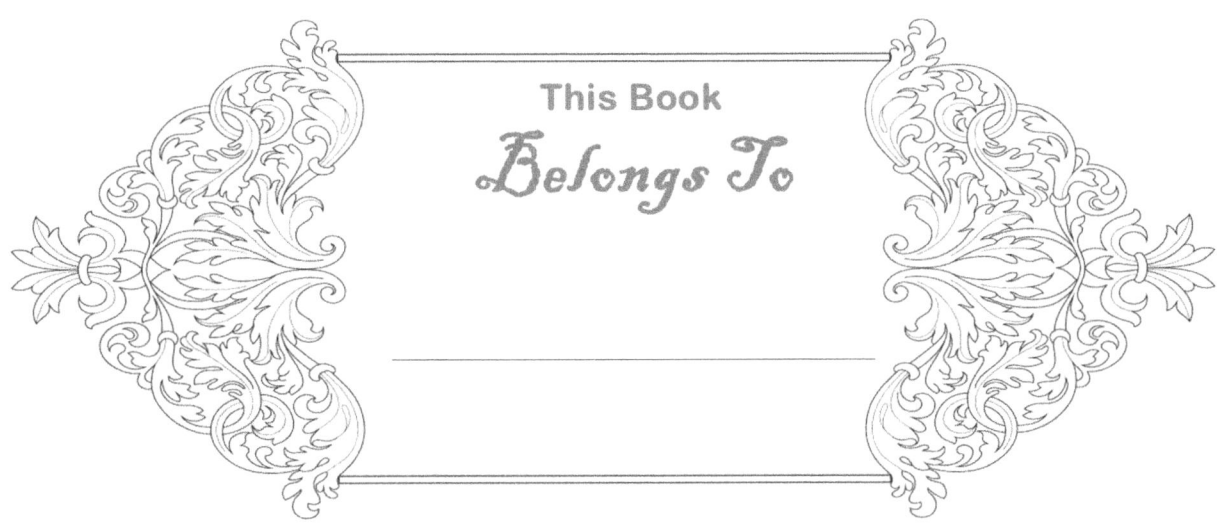

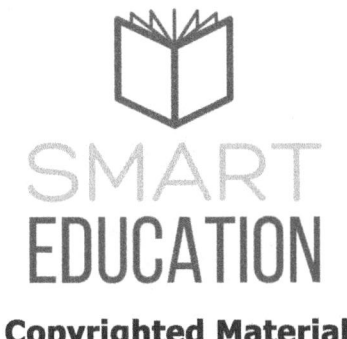

**Copyrighted Material**

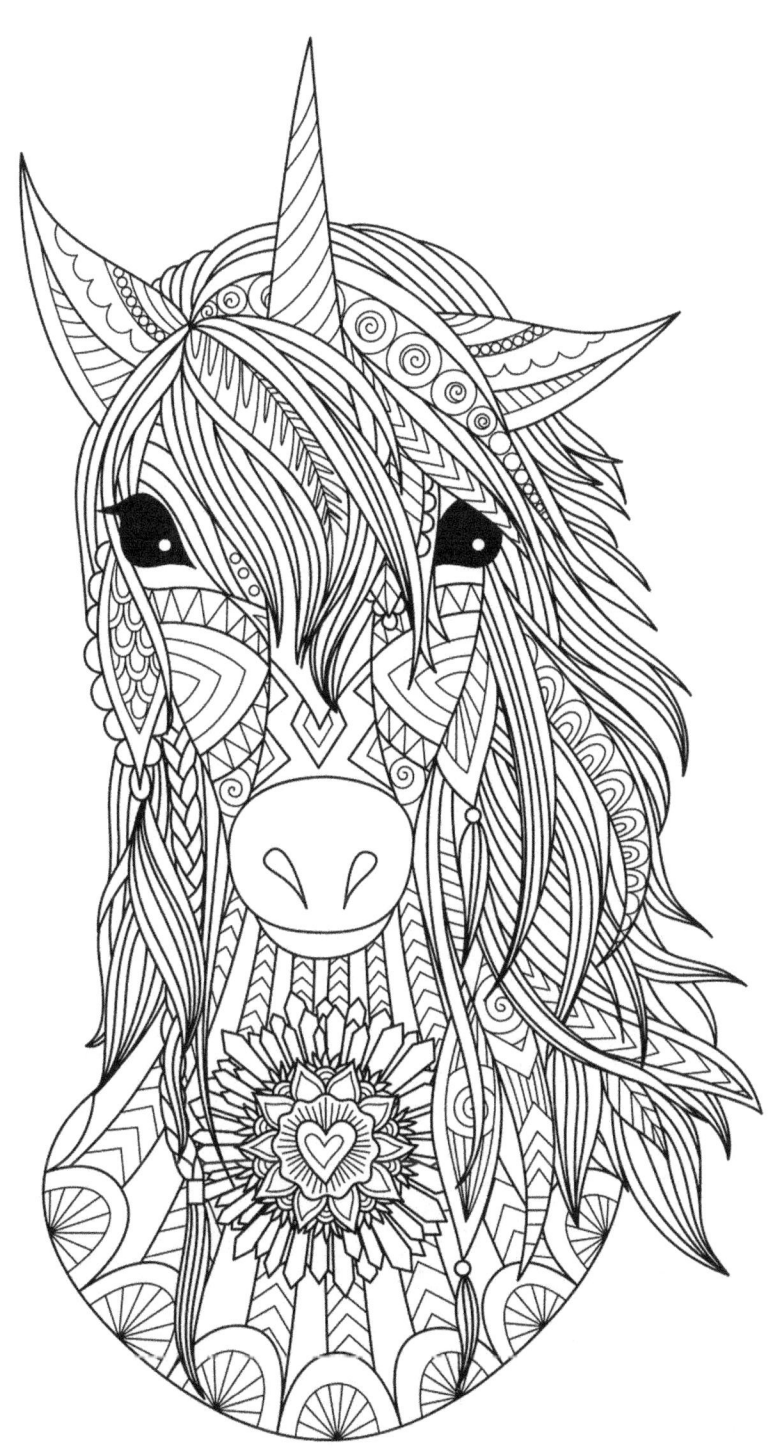

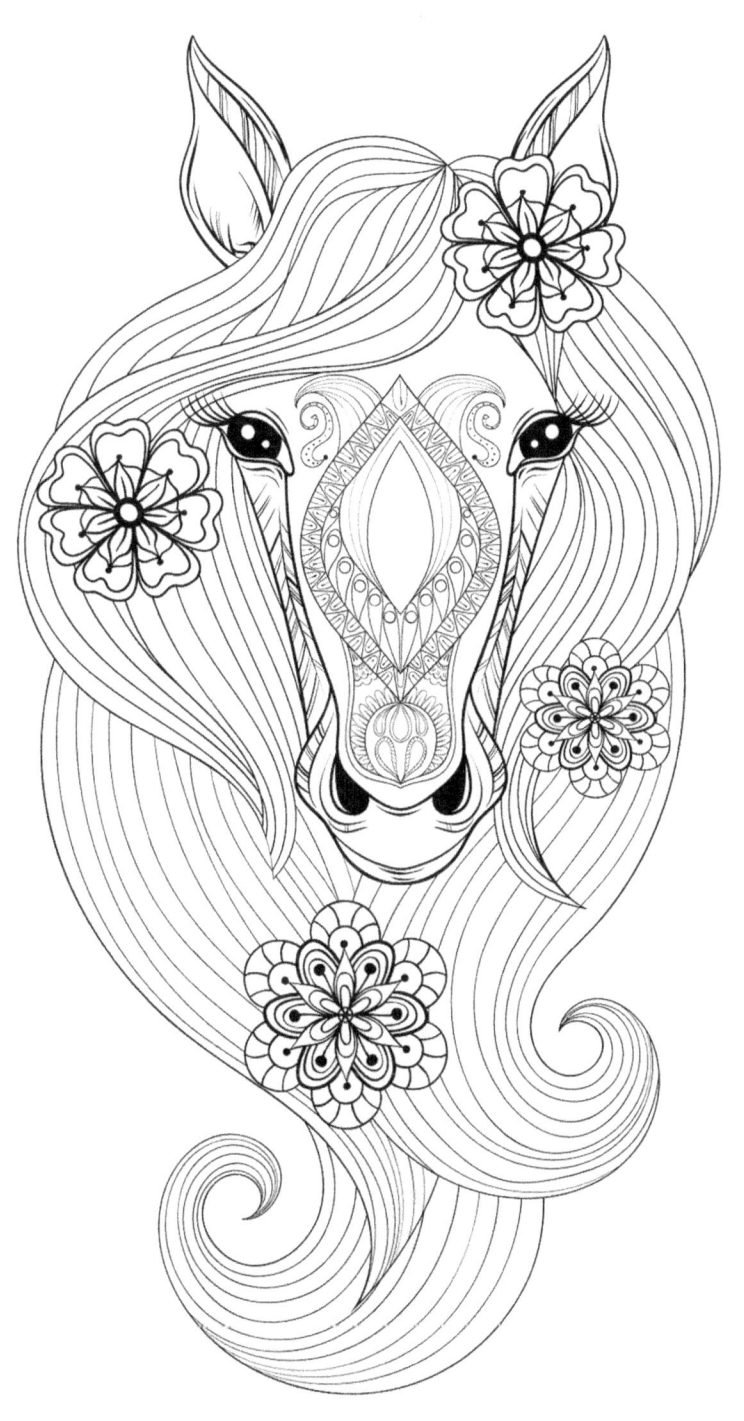

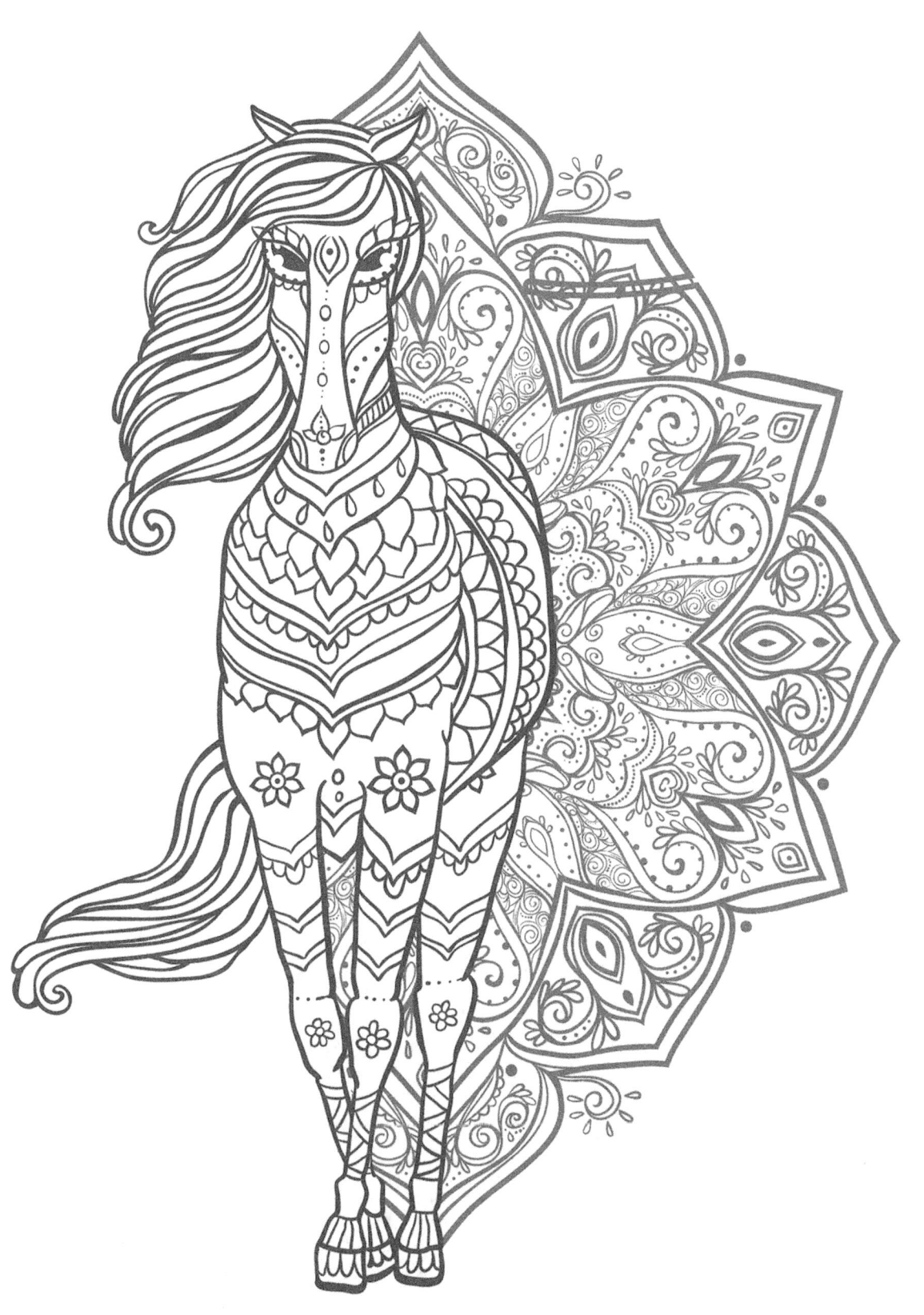

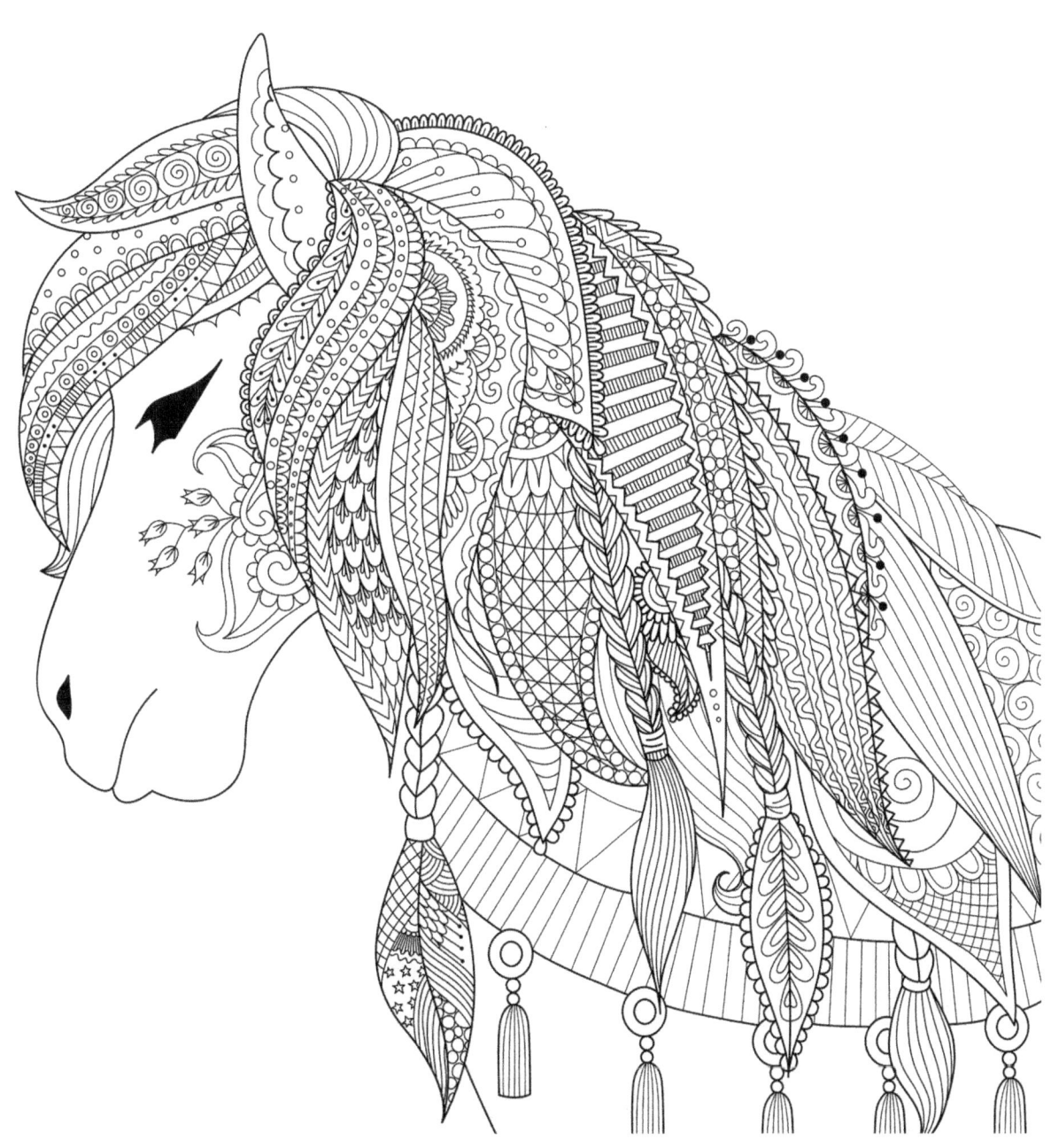

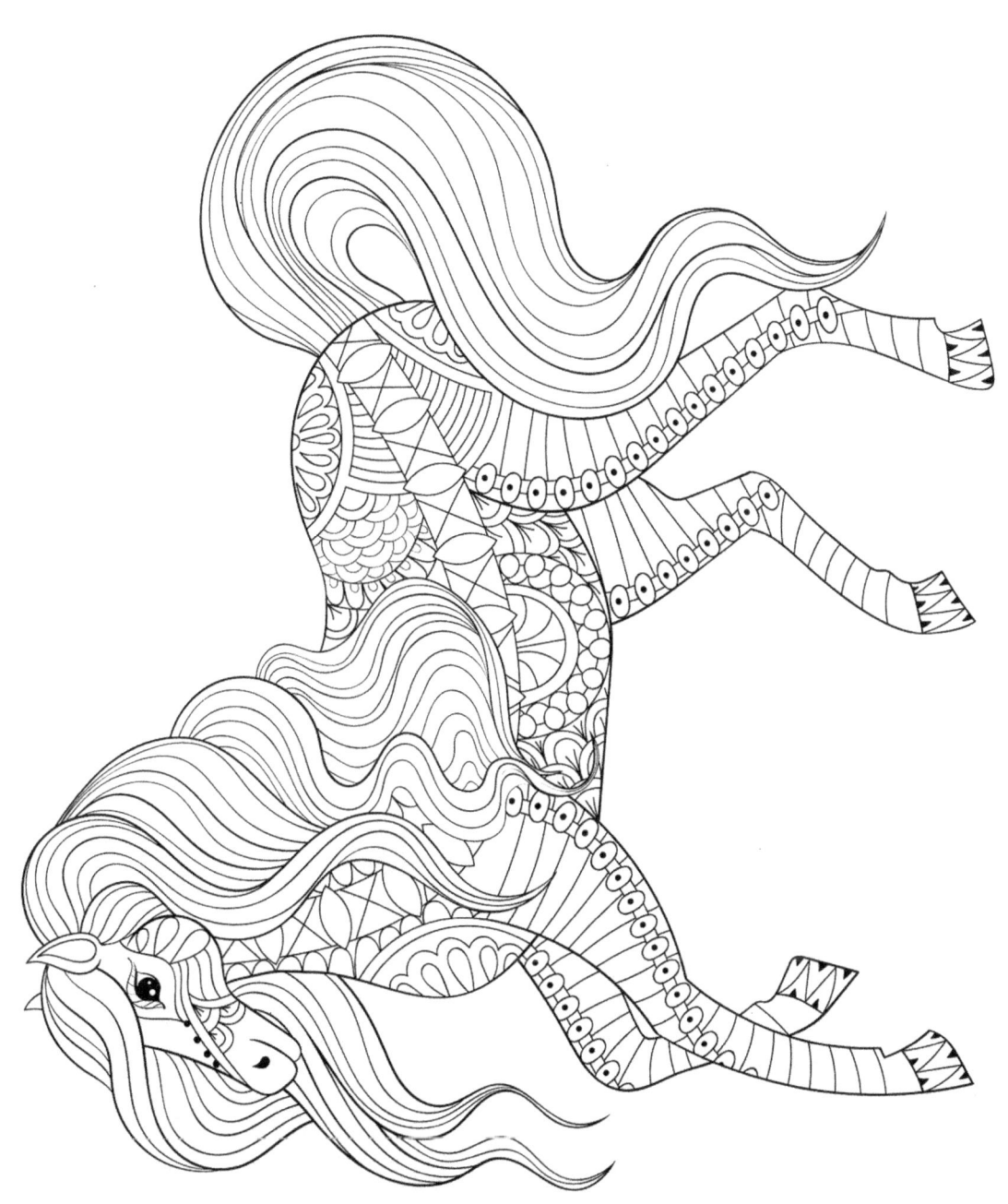

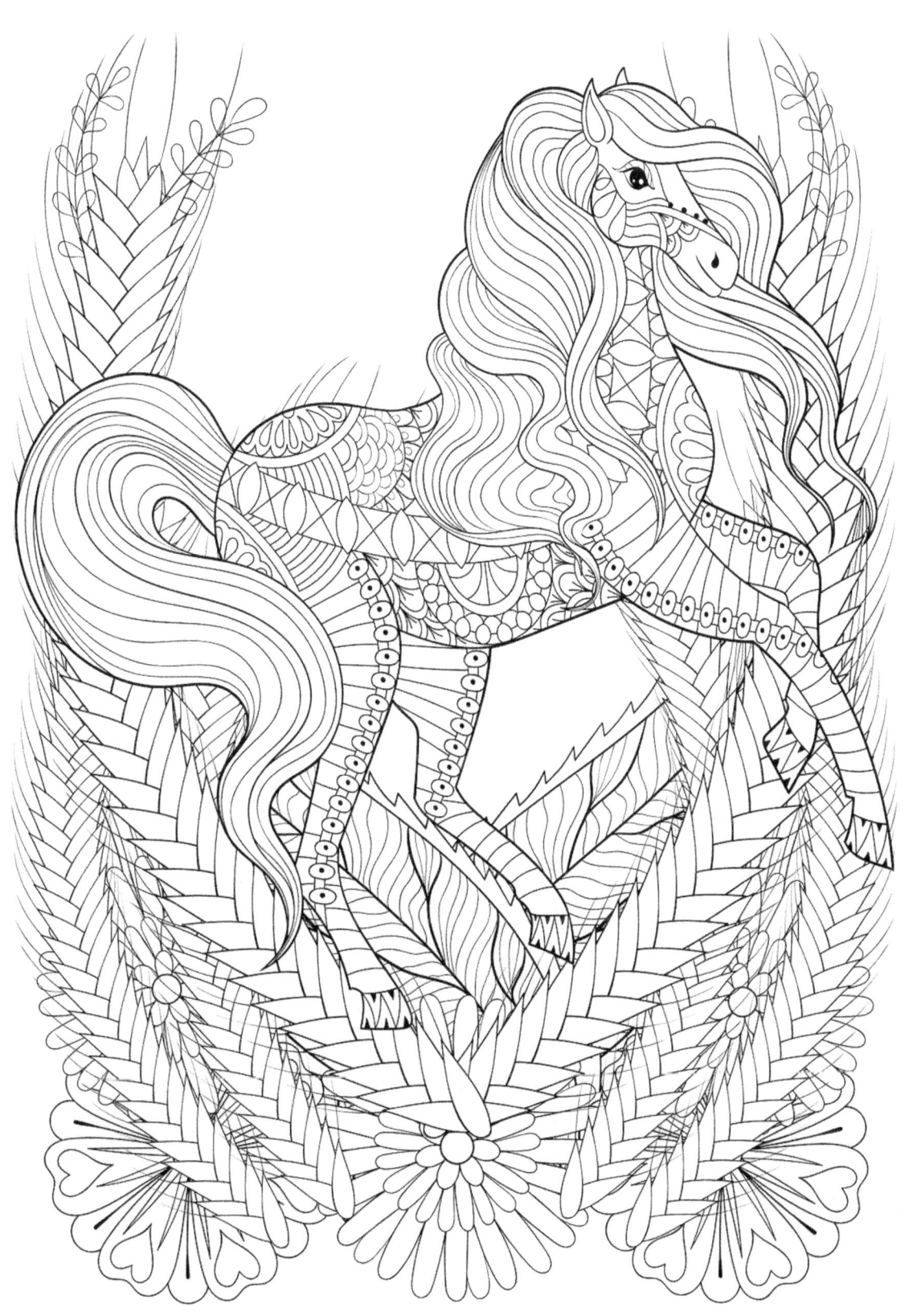

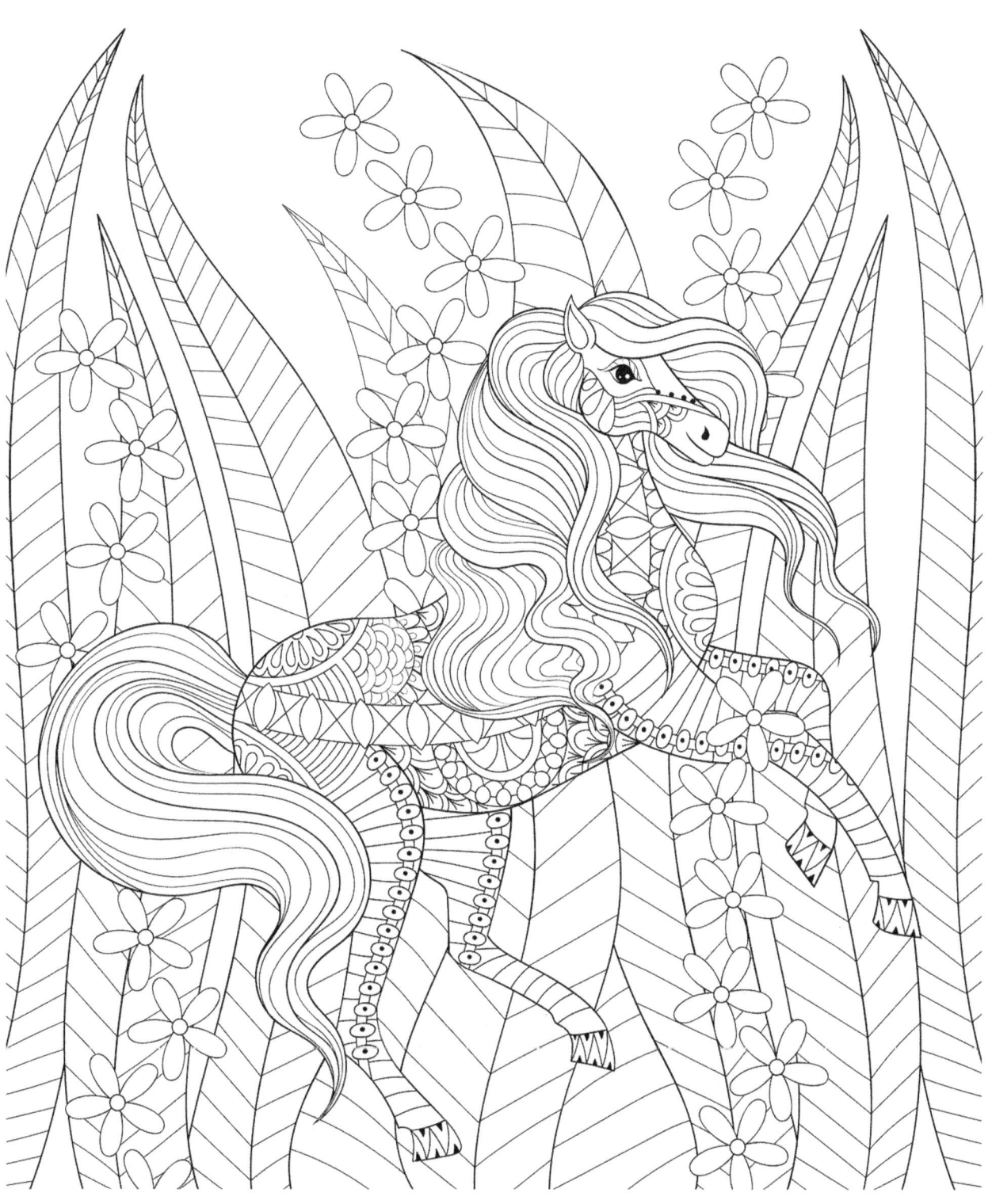

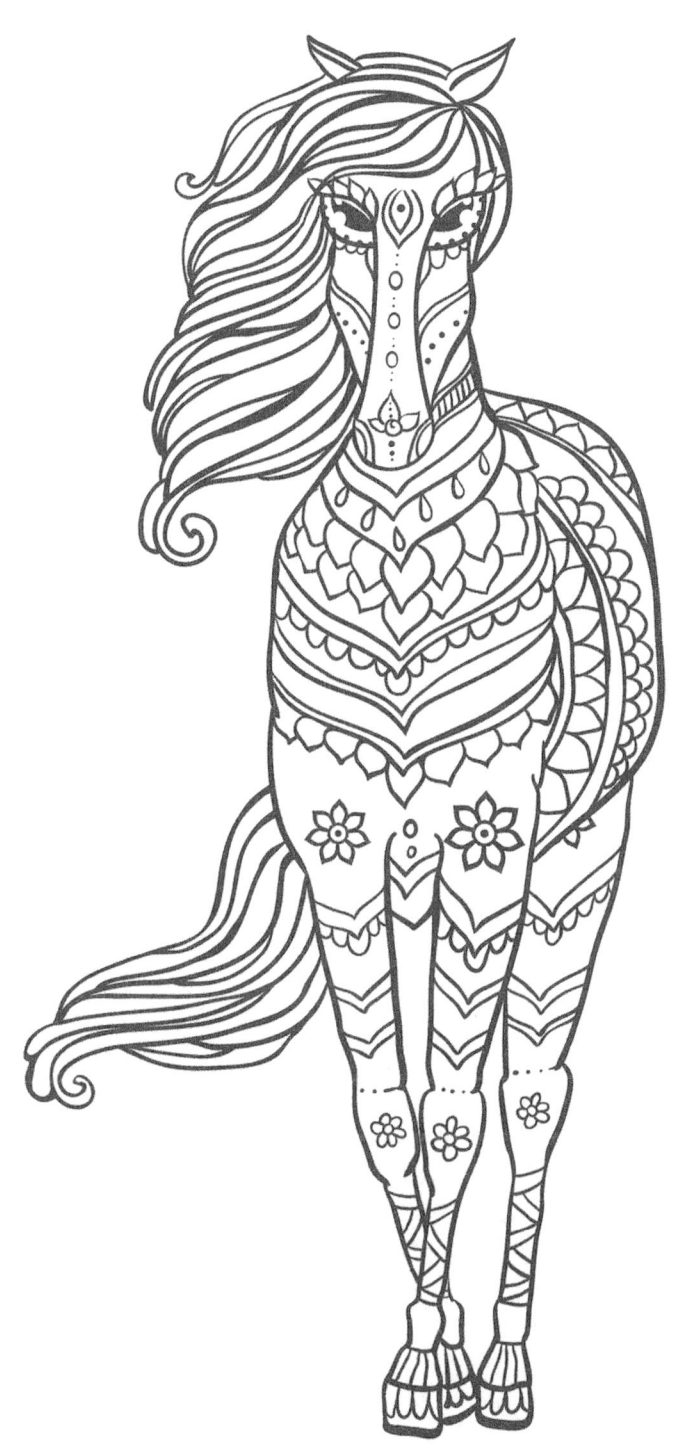

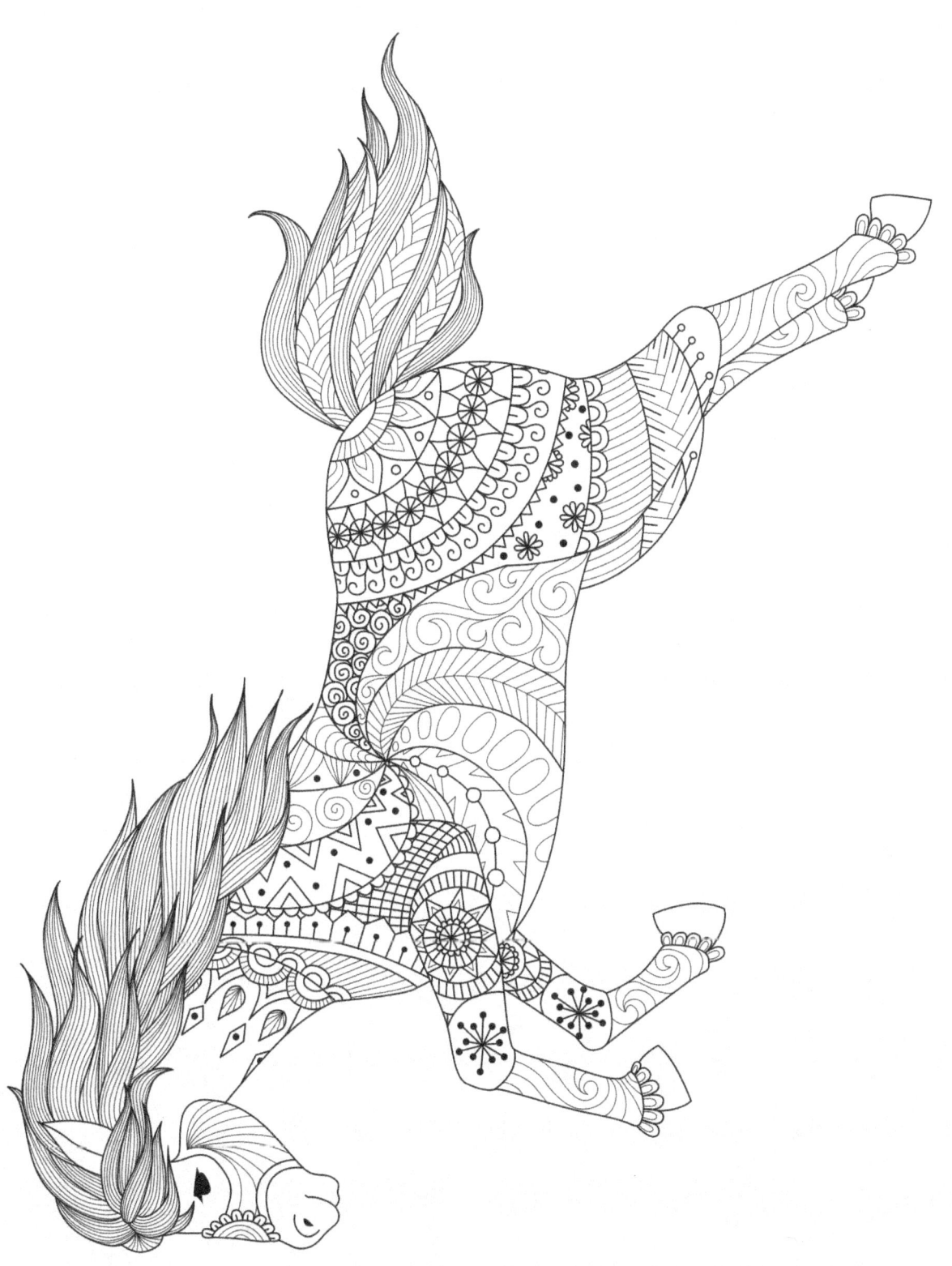

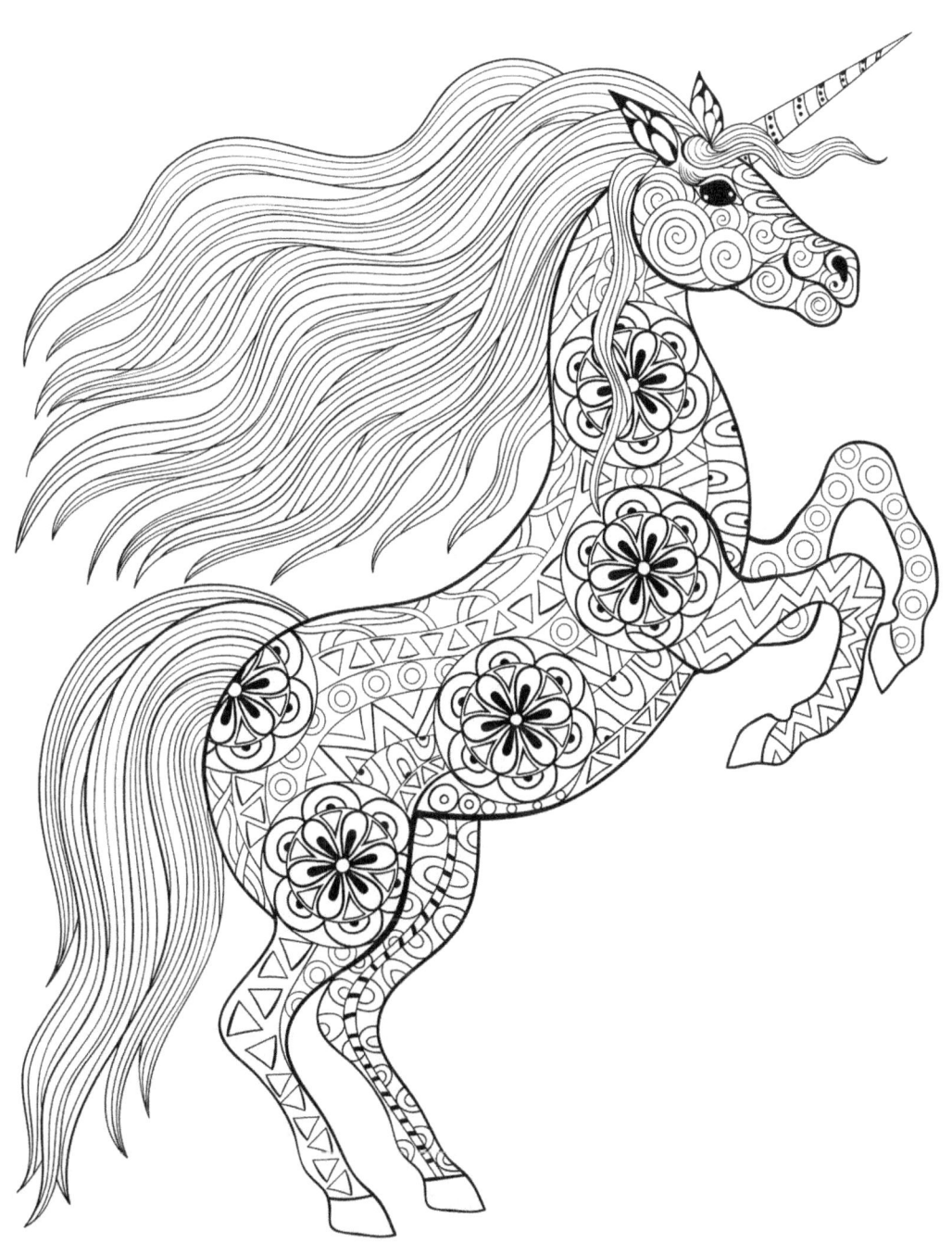

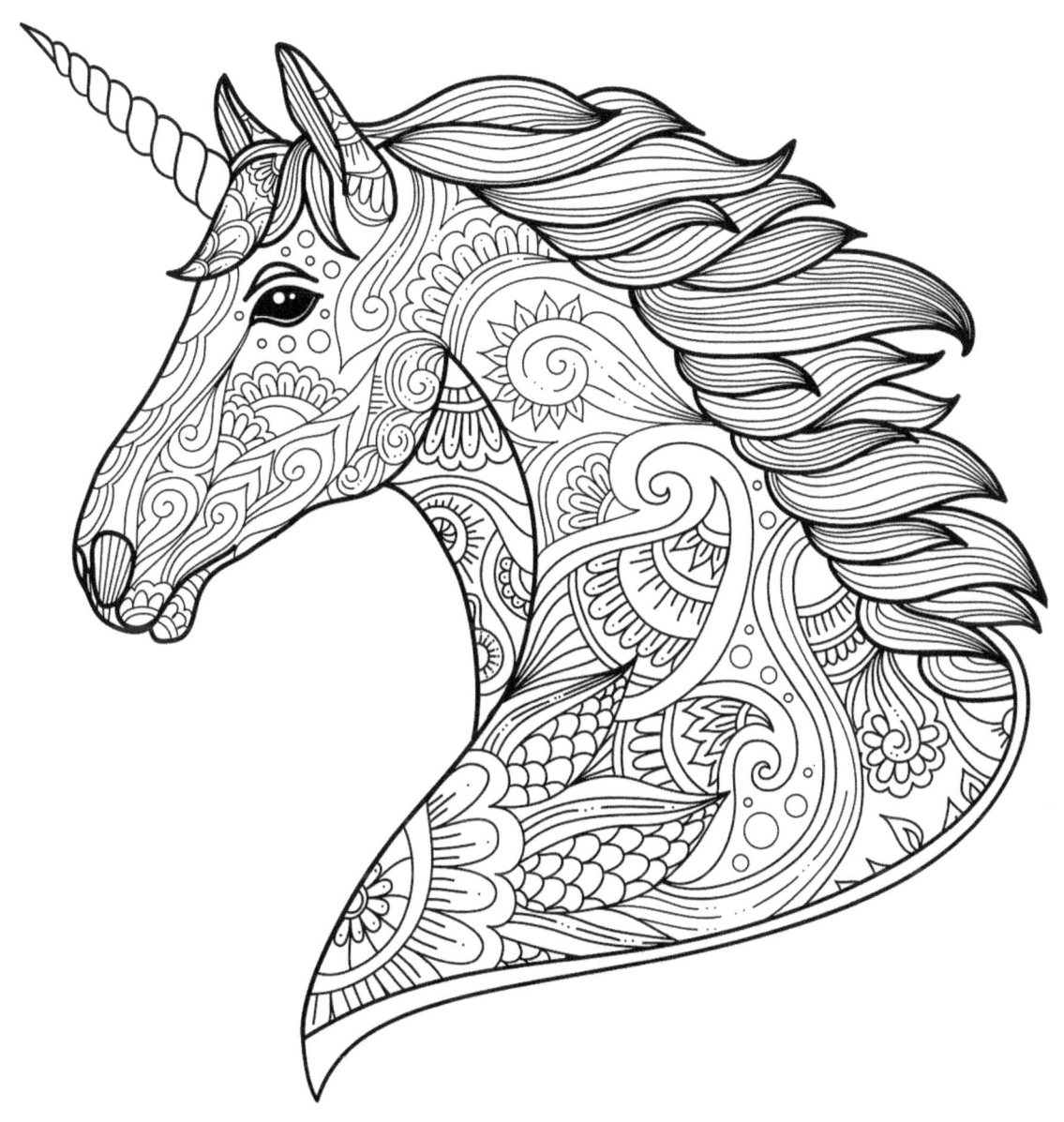

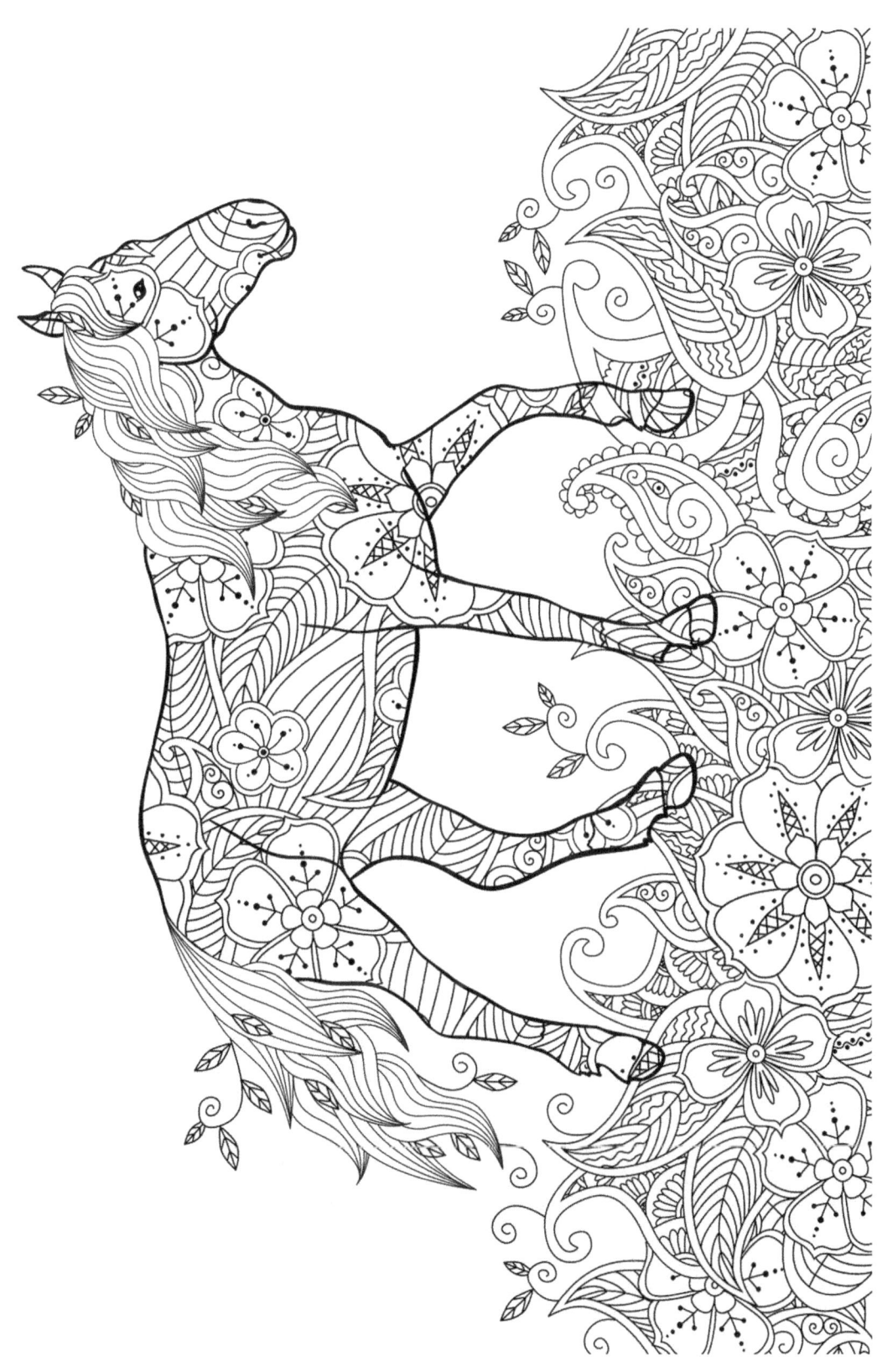

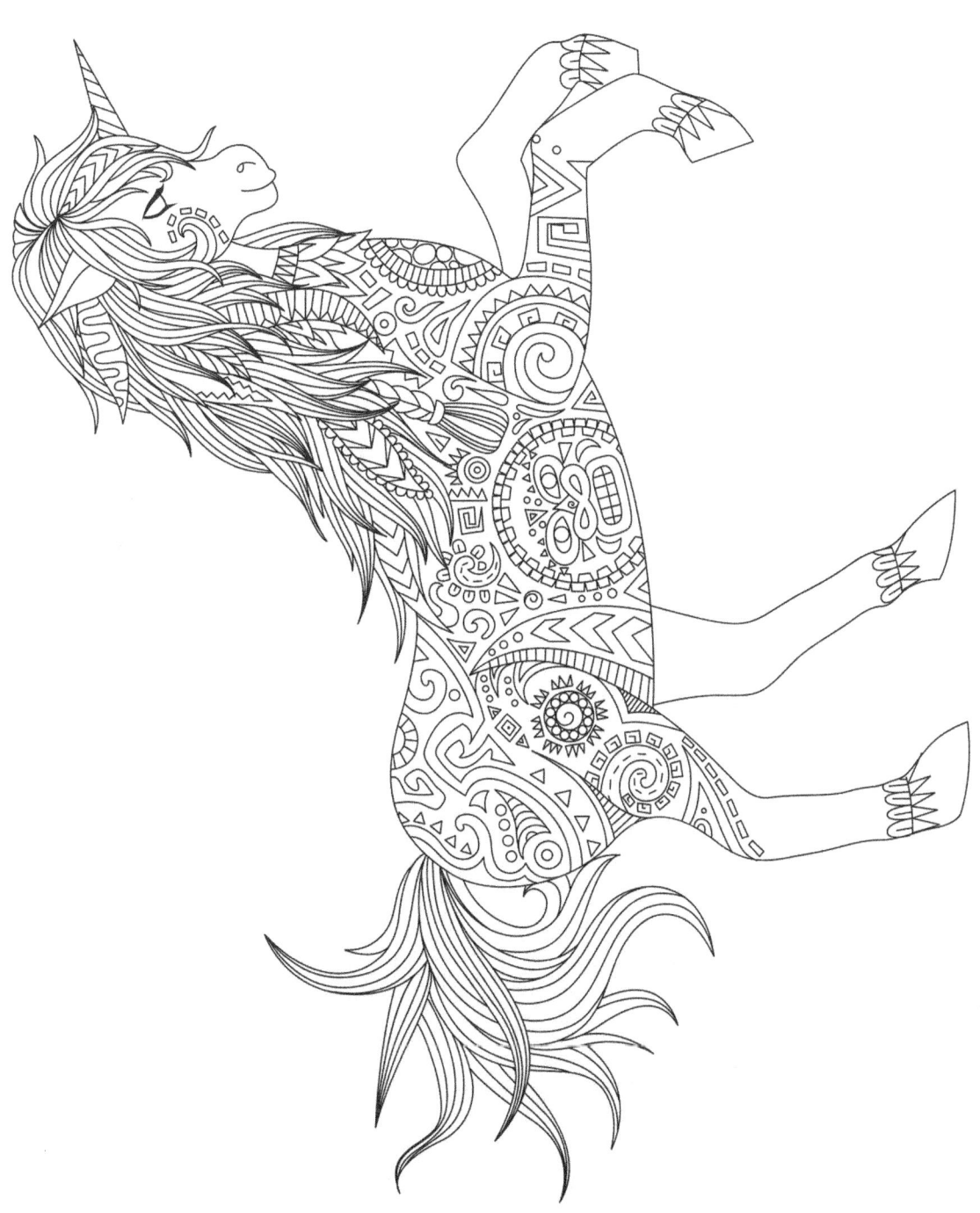

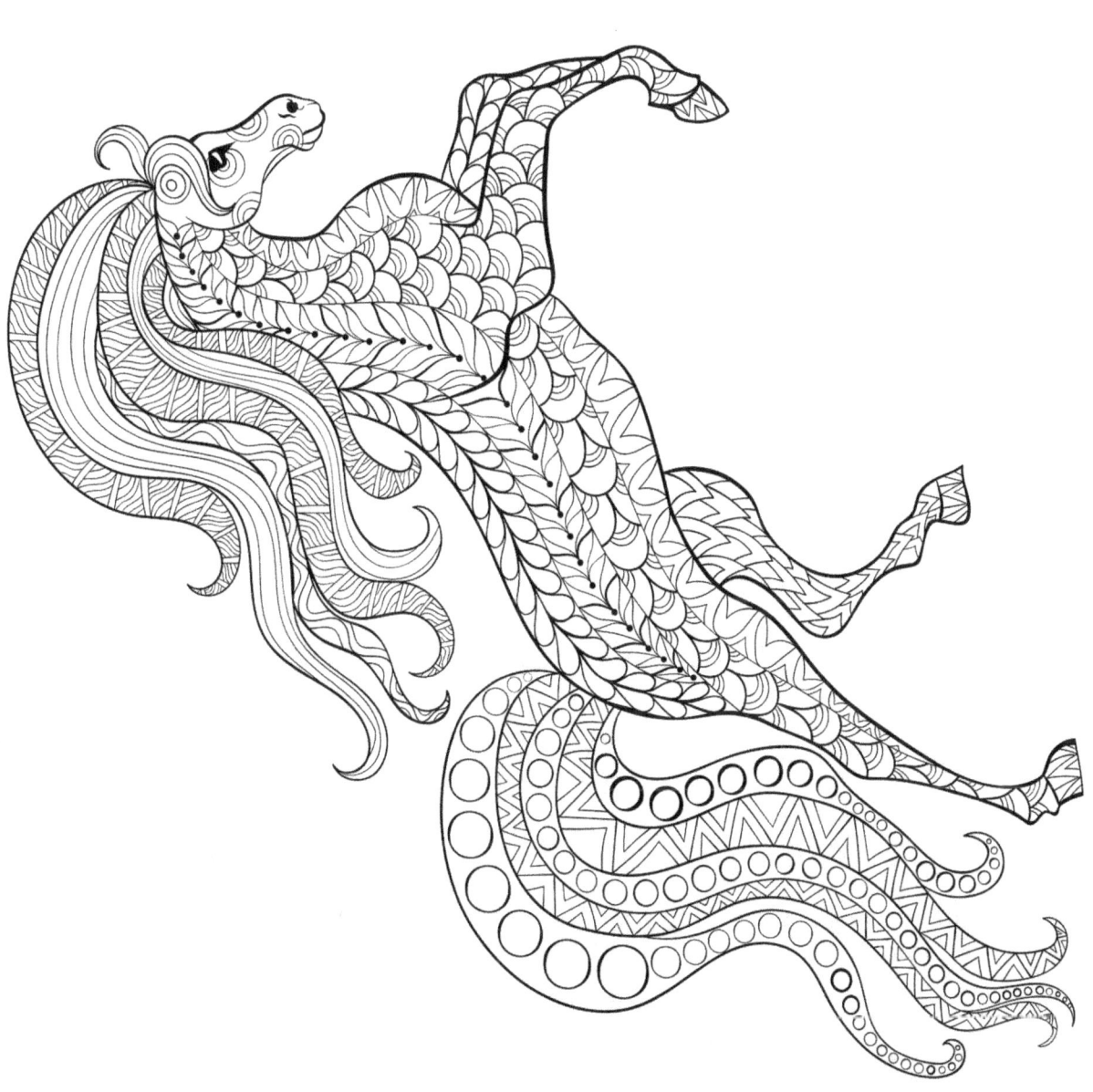

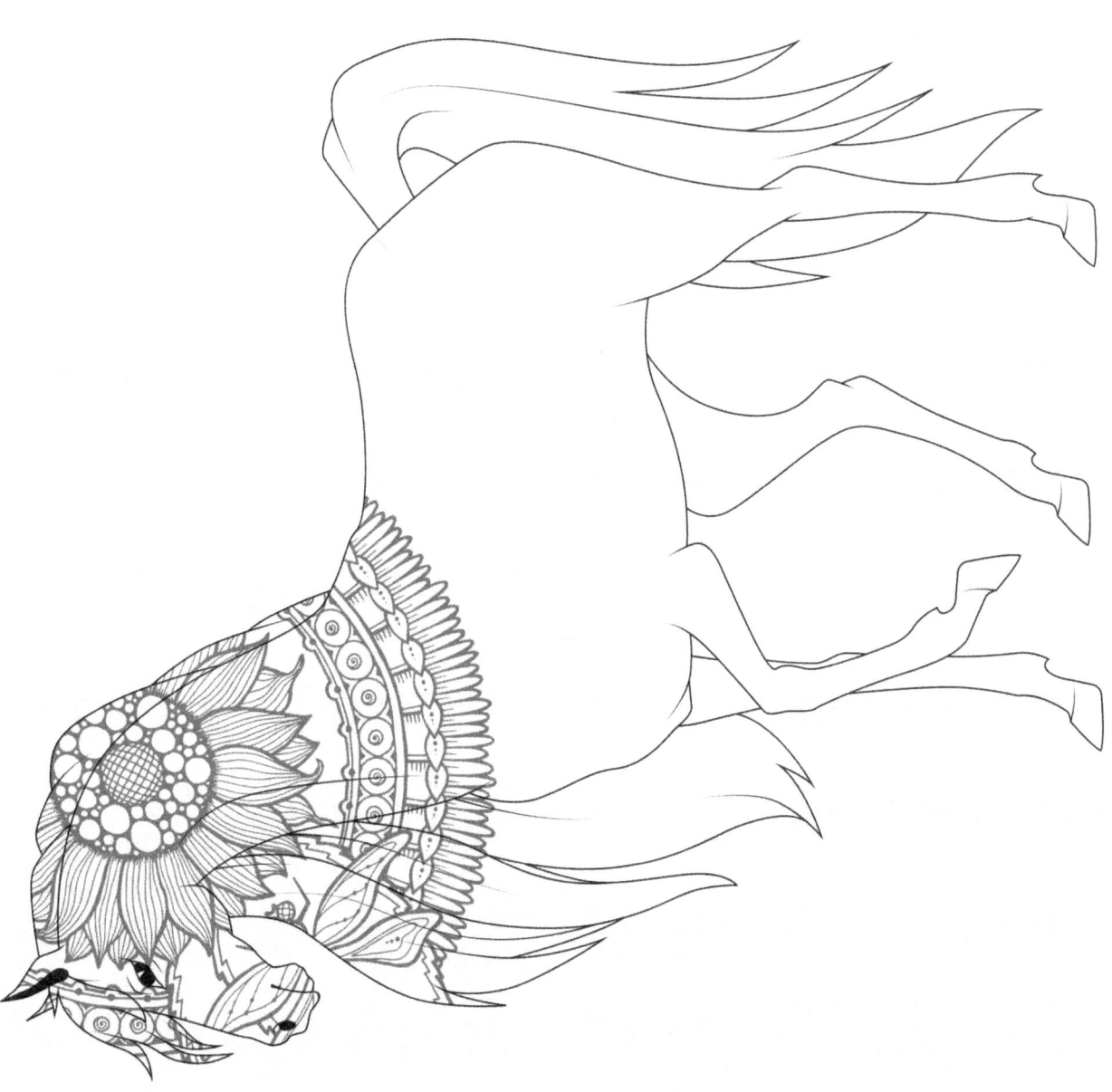

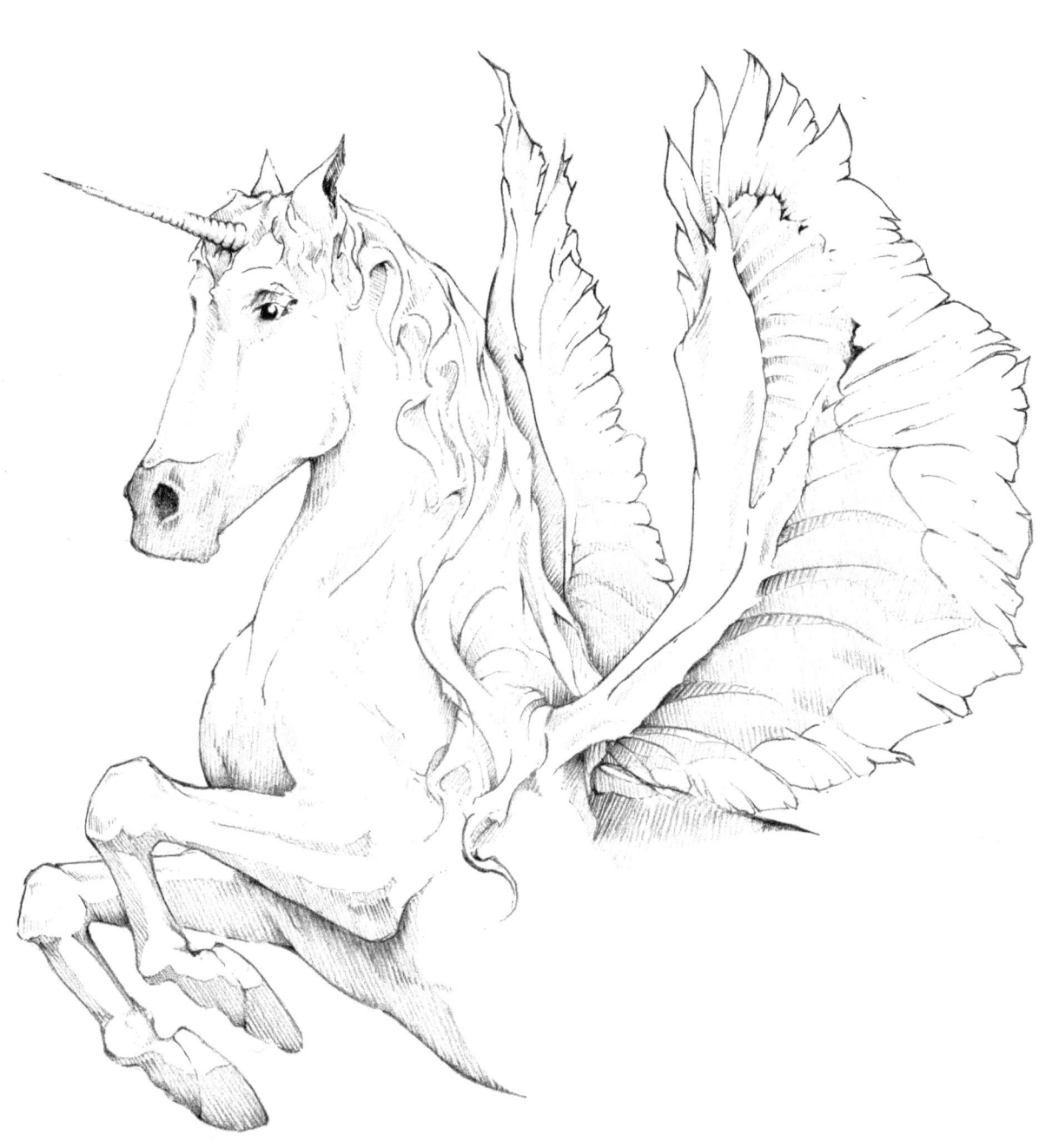

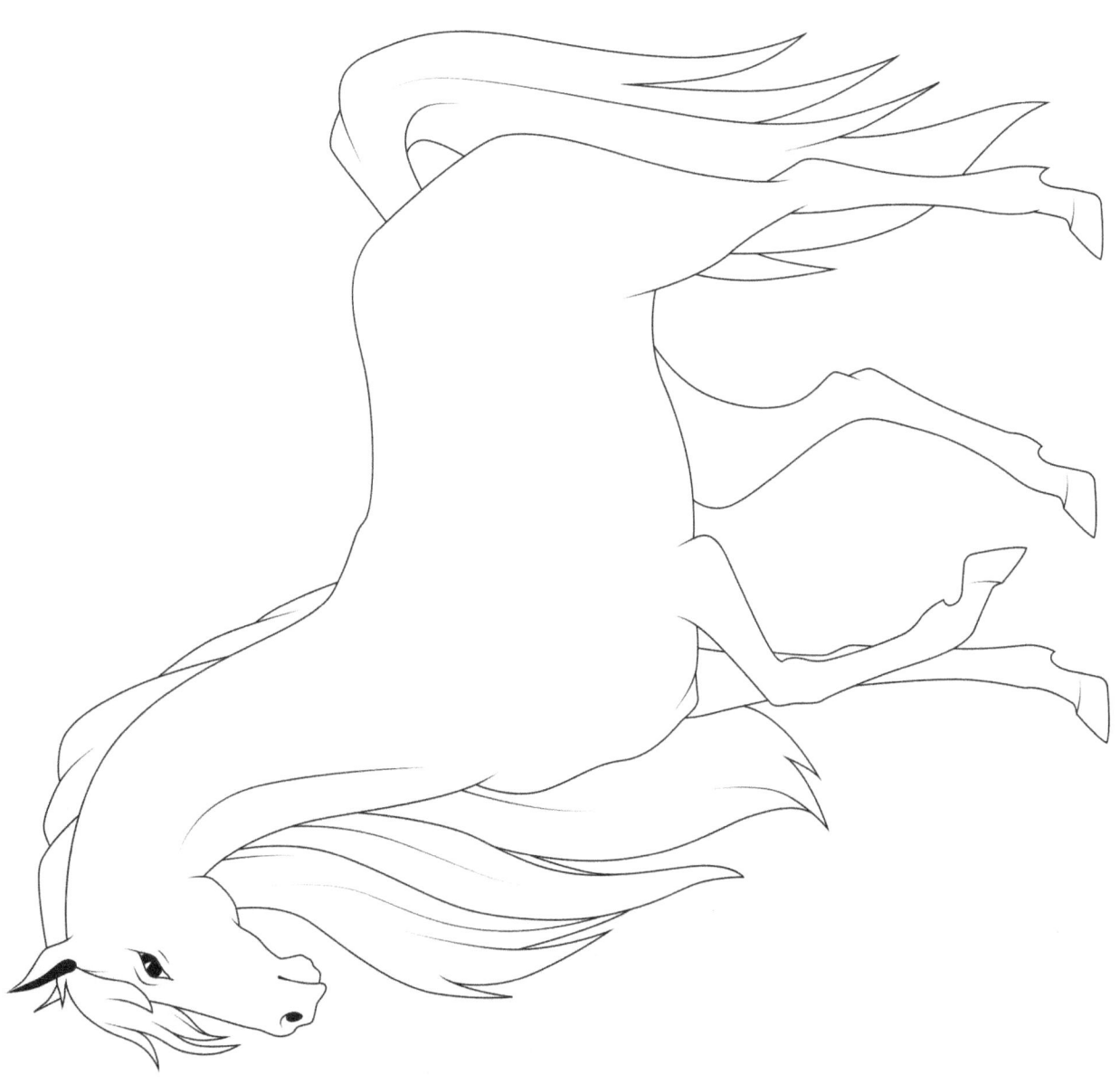

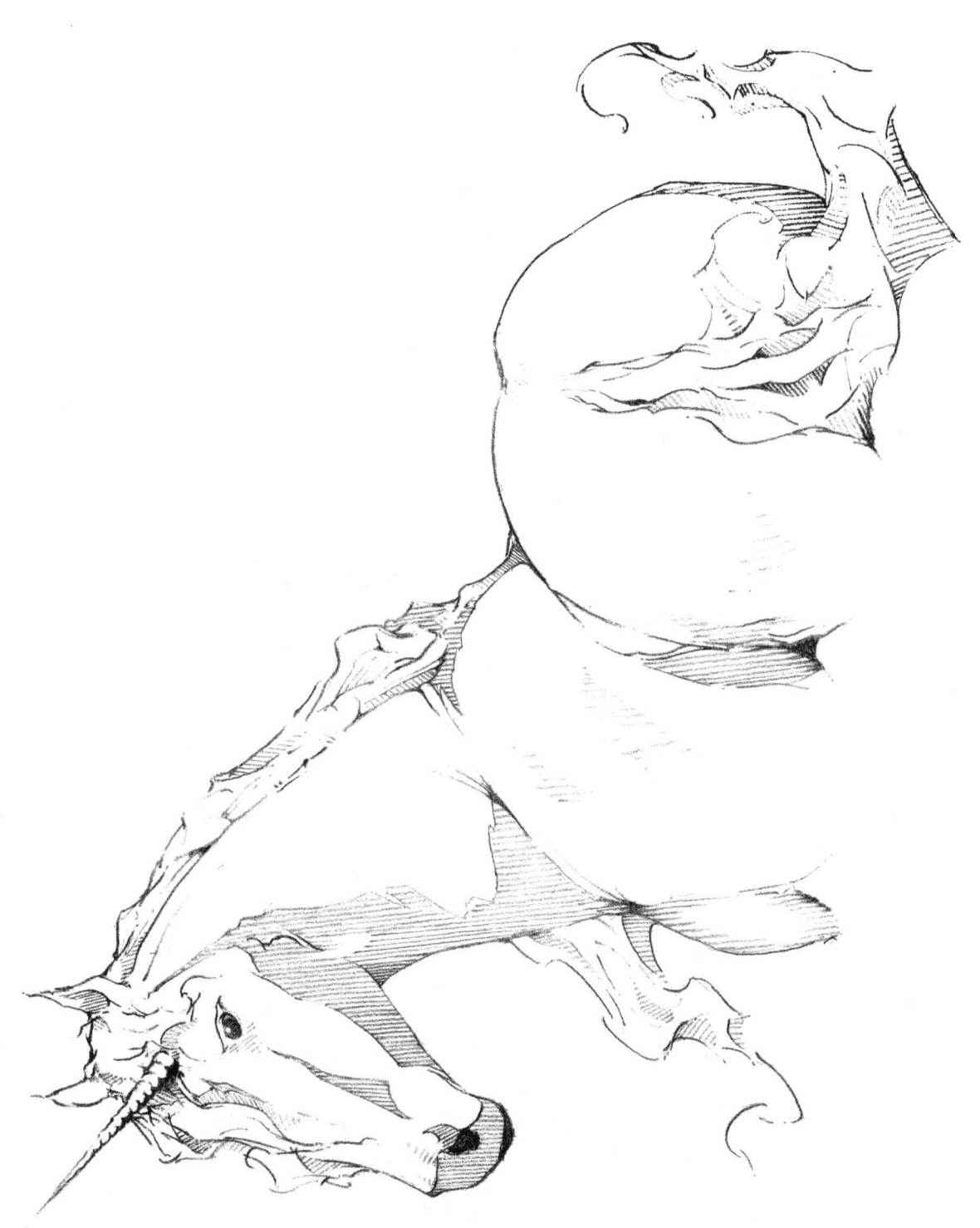

# COLORING BOOKS FOR ADULT

## Animals For relaxation

### Horse Collection

**Follow Us By Click Logo**

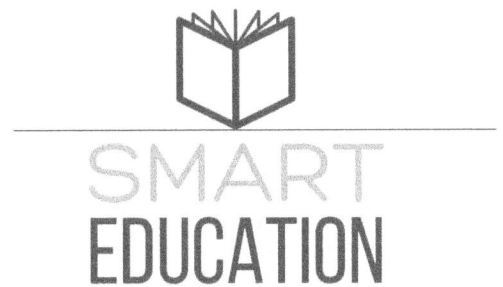

**Copyrighted Material**

www.ingramcontent.com/pod-product-compliance
Lightning Source LLC
Chambersburg PA
CBHW062207220526
45470CB00009B/2950